ABCs
of
Baseball

by **Peter GOLENBOCK**

pictures by **Dan ANDREASEN**

DIAL BOOKS FOR YOUNG READERS ⁂ AN IMPRINT OF PENGUIN GROUP (USA) INC.

For Wendy Grassi, my love, grazie
—P.G.

For Bret
—D.A.

DIAL BOOKS FOR YOUNG READERS
A division of Penguin Young Readers Group
Published by The Penguin Group
Penguin Group (USA) Inc., 375 Hudson Street, New York, NY 10014, U.S.A.
Penguin Group (Canada), 90 Eglinton Avenue East, Suite 700, Toronto, Ontario, Canada M4P 2Y3
(a division of Pearson Penguin Canada Inc.)
Penguin Books Ltd, 80 Strand, London WC2R 0RL, England
Penguin Ireland, 25 St. Stephen's Green, Dublin 2, Ireland (a division of Penguin Books Ltd)
Penguin Group (Australia), 250 Camberwell Road, Camberwell, Victoria 3124,
Australia (a division of Pearson Australia Group Pty Ltd)
Penguin Books India Pvt Ltd, 11 Community Centre, Panchsheel Park, New Delhi - 110 017, India
Penguin Group (NZ), 67 Apollo Drive, Rosedale, Auckland 0632, New Zealand (a division of Pearson New Zealand Ltd)
Penguin Books (South Africa) (Pty) Ltd, 24 Sturdee Avenue, Rosebank, Johannesburg 2196, South Africa
Penguin Books Ltd, Registered Offices: 80 Strand, London WC2R 0RL, England

Designed by Irene Vandervoort and Jasmin Rubero
Text set in Bulmer MT Std with Calvert MT Std
Manufactured in China on acid-free paper

10 9 8 7 6 5 4 3 2 1

Library of Congress Cataloging-in-Publication Data
Golenbock, Peter, date.
ABCs of baseball / by Peter Golenbock ; illustrated by Dan Andreasen.
p.   cm.
ISBN 978-0-8037-3711-2 (hardcover)
1. Baseball—Juvenile literature. 2. Alphabet—Juvenile literature. I. Andreasen, Dan, ill. II. Title.
GV867.5.G65 2012   796.357—dc23   2011021928

INTRODUCTION

Blessed with the baseball gene, I grew up a fan of America's Pastime. As a child I collected baseball cards and memorized the statistics on the back. When I grew older, I was even luckier. I was able to spend most of my life writing about the game and its players.

Baseball can seem hard to understand at times, and the goal of this book is to remove much of the mystery. Here are some of the key rules and terms for baseball fans young and old. Go out to the ballpark, get your peanuts and Cracker Jack, and root, root, root for the home team.

Peter Golenbock
St. Petersburg, Florida

A

Ace: A team's best starting pitcher.

America's Pastime: There's no game like baseball in the world.

April: The month when baseball season begins.

Around the horn: Throwing the ball between three or more infielders during or after a play.

At bat: A hitter's turn to bat.

B

The Babe: Babe Ruth, also called the **Bambino**, is considered one of the greatest baseball players of all time.

Base: There are four: first base, second base, third base, and home plate. If you are standing on one, you can't be tagged out.

Baseball: Covered with white cowhide and 256 red stitches, 9¼ inches in circumference, weighing 5¼ ounces.

Bases loaded: A player from the hitting team on each base.

Bat: Used for hitting the ball.

Batboy: A boy who carries the bats around for a team.

Batting Average: A player's number of hits divided by his number of at bats.

Bleachers: Long benches for the fans. Usually, they're the cheapest tickets in the stadium.

Box score: A printed summary of the game in table form in the newspaper.

Bull pen: The area off the field where pitchers warm up.

Bunt: A short hit achieved by a quick tap of the bat.

C

Can of corn: An easy catch by the fielder.

Cards: For trading or collecting. They've been around since the 1860s.

Alexander Cartwright: The man who invented baseball. He decided the shape of the field and the number of players on each team.

Coaches: During the game they stand near first base and third base and tell the runners what to do.

Cracker Jack: A treat made of caramelized popcorn and peanuts. It has been a staple at baseball games ever since popping up in the 1908 song "Take Me Out to the Ball Game."

Designated hitter: A player who bats in place of another player in the lineup. The American League allows a designated hitter to hit for the pitcher, while the National League does not.

Diamond: The shape of the infield where baseball is played, made by the four bases spaced exactly ninety feet apart.

Double: A hit that allows the batter to reach second base safely.

Double play: When two outs are scored in the same play.

Dugout: Where players sit during the game when they're not out on the field.

ERA: stands for **Earned Run Average**. It's a number showing how many runs a pitcher gives up per nine innings. The lower the ERA, the better the pitcher.

Error: A missed play or mistake— such as a player letting the ball go through his legs or throwing it into the stands—that allows the runner to advance.

Extra innings: When the nine innings in a game end in a tie, teams must play more until one of them scores. Also called **free baseball**.

Fans: People who follow and root, root, root for a team.

Fielder's choice: Term used when a fielder can choose among base runners to throw or tag out.

Flag: It waves atop the pole in center field.

Fly ball: A batted ball that goes high in the air.

Foul ball: A ball that lands outside the foul—or white—lines on the field.

Glove: The leather mitt that players use to catch the ball.

Grand Slam: A home run with the bases loaded.

Green grass: What the baseball field is made of. Some stadiums where the game is played inside use an imitation playing surface that looks like grass.

Green light: A signal from the third base coach to a base runner that tells him to continue running.

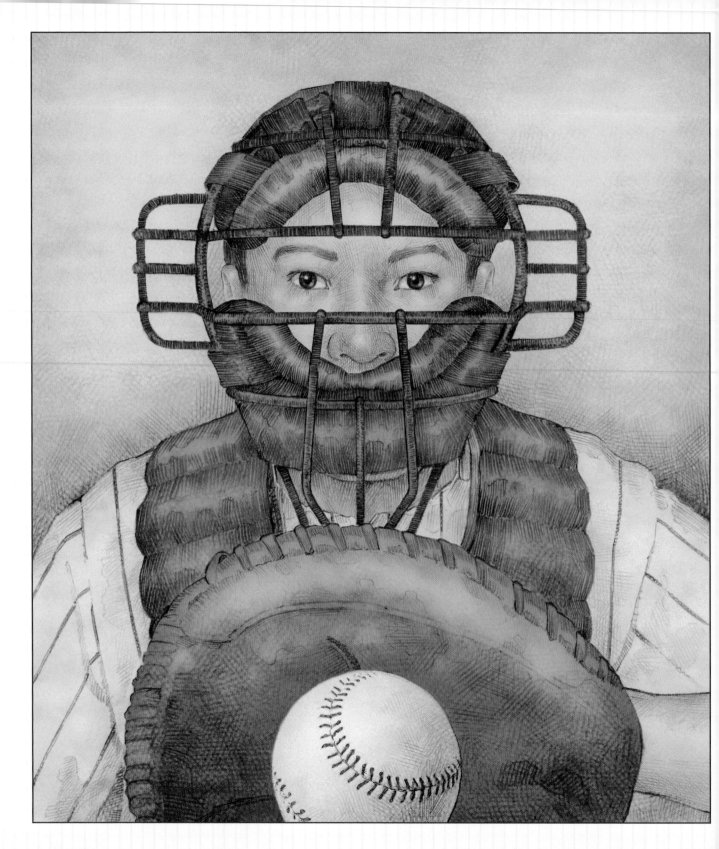

Hall of Fame: The place where baseball commemorates its greatest players.

Hit: When a batter reaches a base safely after landing the ball in fair territory.

Home plate: The base where the hitters bat or runners tag for a run.

Home run: A long hit where the ball goes fair into the stands and the hitter tags all the bases and scores.

Hot corner: A nickname for third base.

Hot dog: What baseball fans love to eat.

I

Infield: The area inside the baseball diamond. The infield positions are first, second, and third baseman, as well as shortstop.

Inning: The main division of a game. Each team gets to bat and make three outs, and there are nine total in a game.

J

Jersey: Every player wears one as the top part of his team uniform.

Joy: What you feel watching the game.

K: Short for **Strikeout** on the scorecard.

League: A grouping of teams. Major League Baseball is divided into the **American League** and the **National League**, and each league has an East, a West, and a Central division.

Line drive: A hit that is hard and straight.

Lineup: The nine starting players on the team in the order they bat.

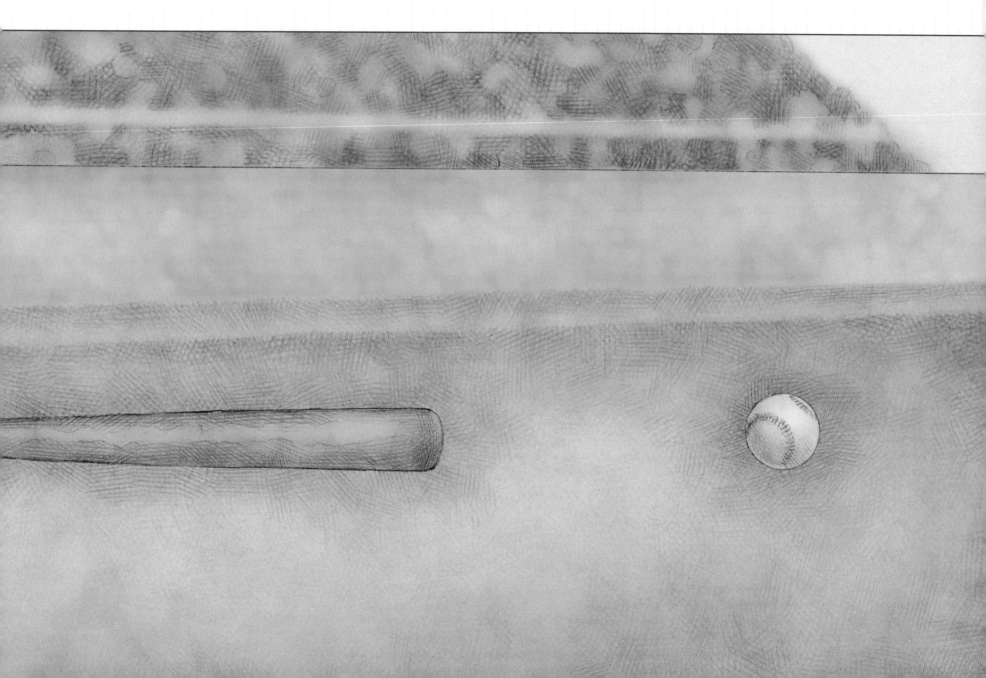

Manager: The man who runs the team and picks the lineups.

Minor league: A step just below the major league, where players can get professional field time while trying to move up to the major league.

Mound: The raised circle in the middle of the field where the pitcher stands.

Negro League: Until 1947, when Jackie Robinson joined the Brooklyn Dodgers, African-American baseball players were not permitted to play in the major leagues. They played in their own leagues.

No-hitter: A game in which one team prevents the other from getting a single hit. If a pitcher pitches the whole game, he has thrown a no-hitter.

O

On deck: The next batter up in the inning. The batter stands in a circular area and warms up before batting.

Opening day: The wonderful, exciting first day of the season.

Out: When a runner gets tagged with the ball, or when a runner reaches a base after the ball gets there.

Outfield: The grassy area beyond the baseball diamond. The outfield positions are left fielder, right fielder, and center fielder.

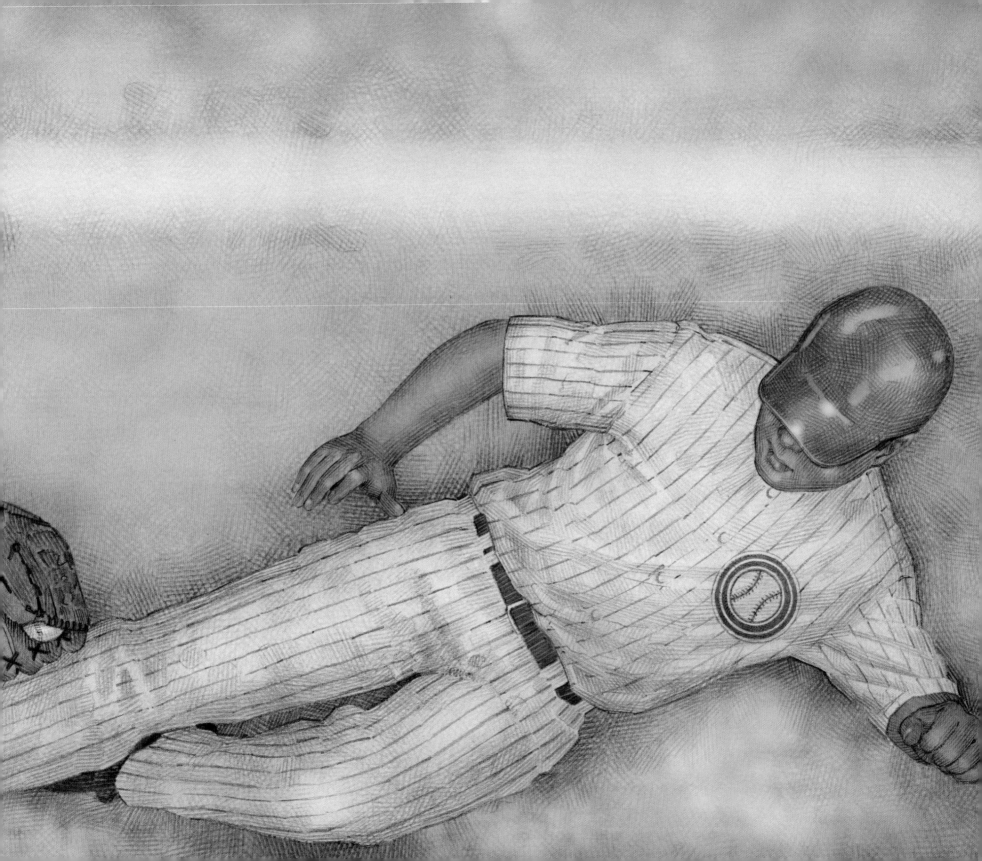

Peanuts: Along with Cracker Jack, a favorite food to eat at a ball game.

Pennant: The prize for the team that wins in its league.

Pinch hitter: A substitute batter who switches places with a player for the rest of the game

Pinch runner: A substitute runner who switches places with a runner on base and then stays in the game.

Pitcher: The player on the mound who throws the ball to the batter and tries to get him out.

Play ball!: What the umpire calls to start the ball game.

Pop-up: A ball hit high up in the air.

Questions: What young fans ask grown-ups at the game.

Quotations: What the players tell reporters.

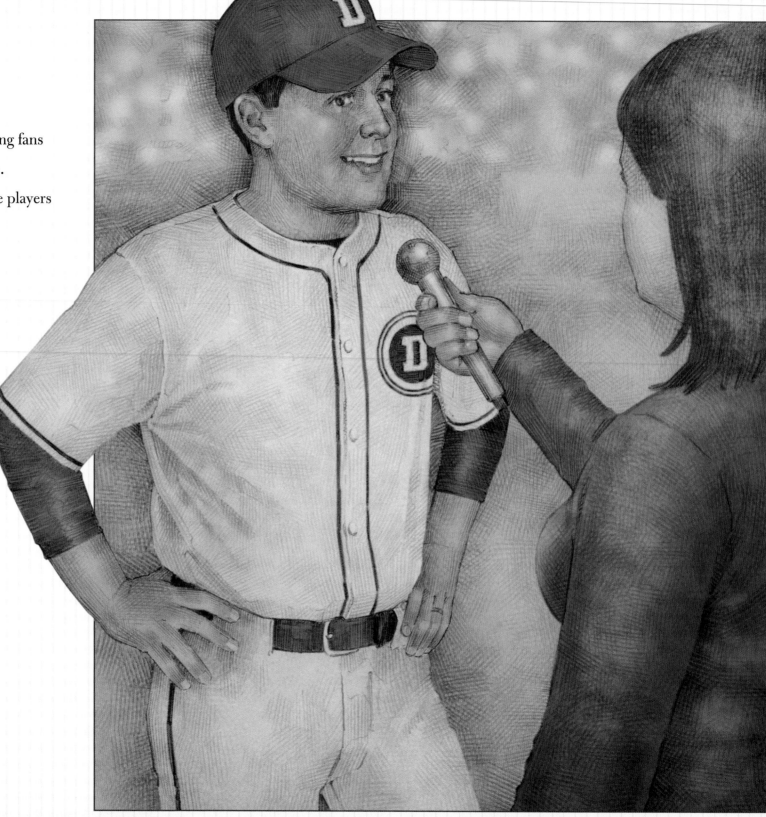

RBI: Stands for **Run Batted In**. If a batter gets a hit and a runner on base comes around to score, the batter receives an RBI.

Relief pitcher: A pitcher who takes over in a game when the starting pitcher gets tired or injured.

Retired number: A player's number that is no longer used on jerseys out of respect to the player who used to have that number.

Rookie: A player who is playing his first season in the major leagues.

Safe!: What the umpire calls when a runner reaches the base before the ball.

Scoreboard: The big sign in the stadium where the score and other statistics are shown.

Season: The 162 games that each team plays each year. The season lasts from April to September, with the post-season tournament in October.

Seventh Inning Stretch: Between halves of the seventh inning, fans take a break to stretch, get food, and sing "Take Me Out to the Ball Game."

Shutout: When a pitcher pitches a game with no runs scored.

Single: A hit that allows the batter to reach first base safely.

Slide: A base runner drops to the ground and skids into a base to get there without getting tagged out.

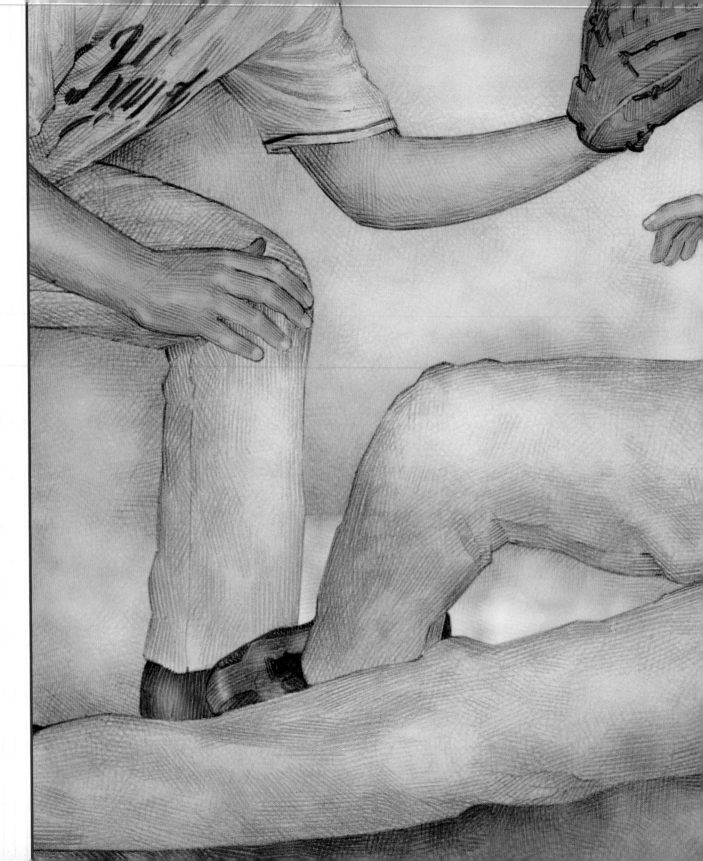

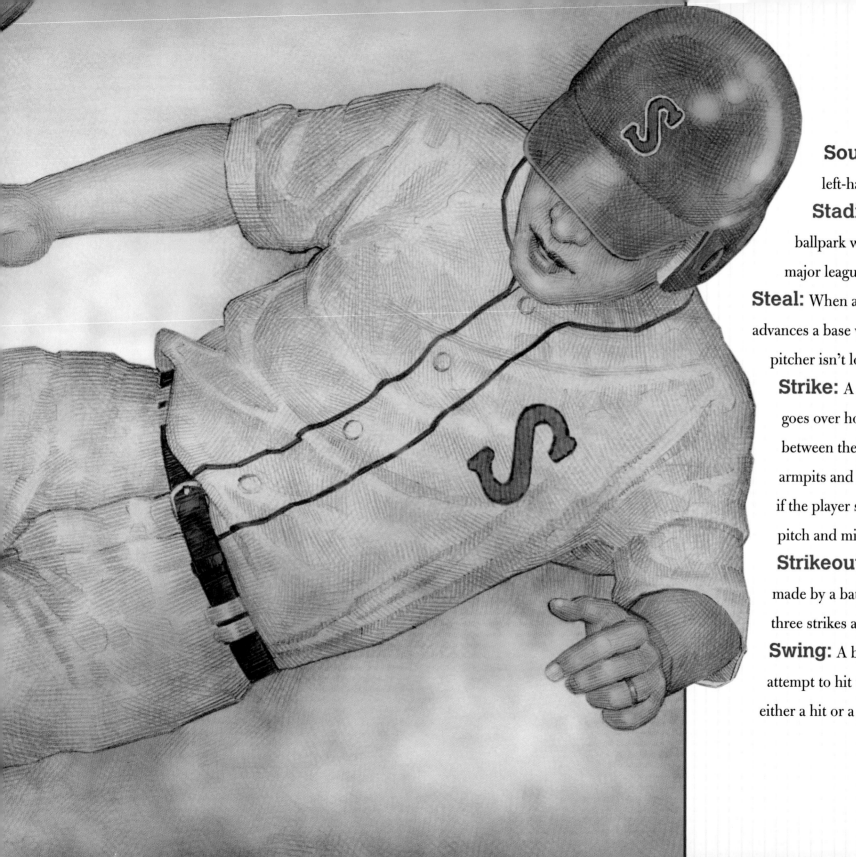

Southpaw: A left-handed pitcher.

Stadium: A big ballpark where the major league teams play.

Steal: When a runner advances a base while the pitcher isn't looking.

Strike: A pitch that goes over home plate between the player's armpits and his knees. Or if the player swings at the pitch and misses it.

Strikeout: An out made by a batter who has three strikes against him.

Swing: A batter's attempt to hit the ball. It is either a hit or a miss!

Team: A baseball team has nine players. Major League Baseball teams can carry twenty-five players altogether, including starting players, bench players, and pitchers.

Ticket: It gets you into the stadium.

Triple: A hit that allows the batter to reach third base safely.

Triple Crown: When a batter leads his league in home runs, RBIs, and batting average for the season, or when a pitcher leads in ERA, wins, and strikeouts.

Triple play: When the fielding team scores all three outs in one play.

Umpires: Officials who call balls, strikes, and outs. Without them, the players would fight all the time.

Uniform: The distinctive outfit worn by the members of a team.

Utility player: A player who plays many positions.

Valuable in **Most Valuable Player:** The MVP has the best performance, effort, and attitude for the season.

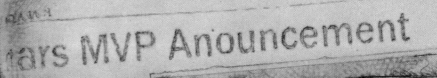

Walk: When the pitcher throws four balls out of the strike zone in an at bat, the batter gets to walk to first base. Sometimes the pitcher will throw an intentional walk if he's afraid the batter will score a run.

Whiff: When a batter swings and misses and strikes out.

Wild pitch: A pitch far away from the strike zone that the catcher cannot catch or block, allowing any base runner to run to the next base.

World Series: When the winning teams from each league play for the championship in October.

X: Looks like the stitches in your glove.

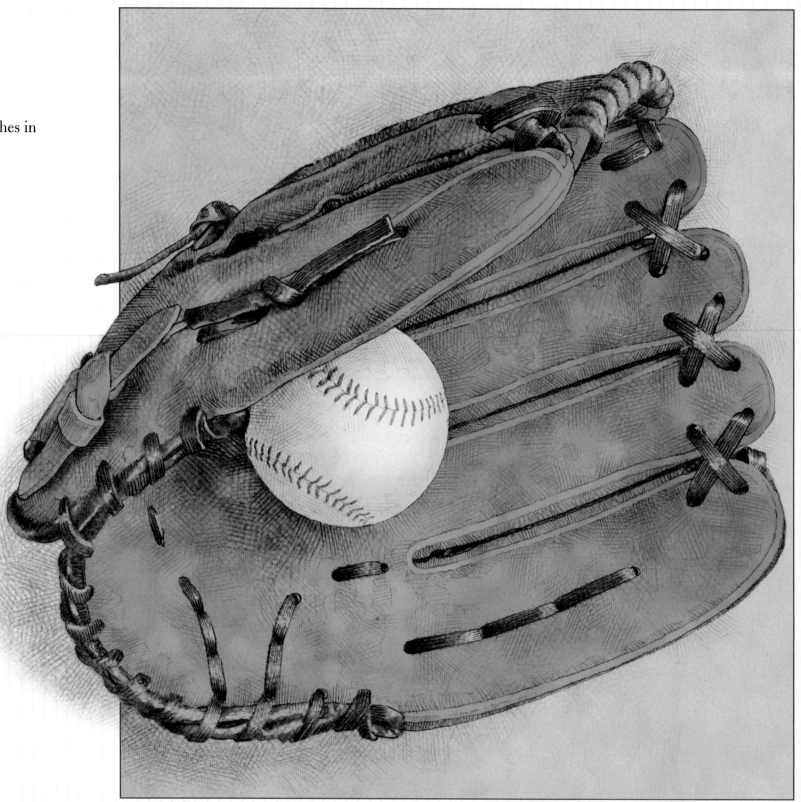

Y'er out!: What the umpire says when the runner fails to reach the base before the ball. Sometimes it's a close call!

Zone: The strike zone is the area over home plate between the batter's armpits and his knees. If the pitch is in this area, it is called a strike.

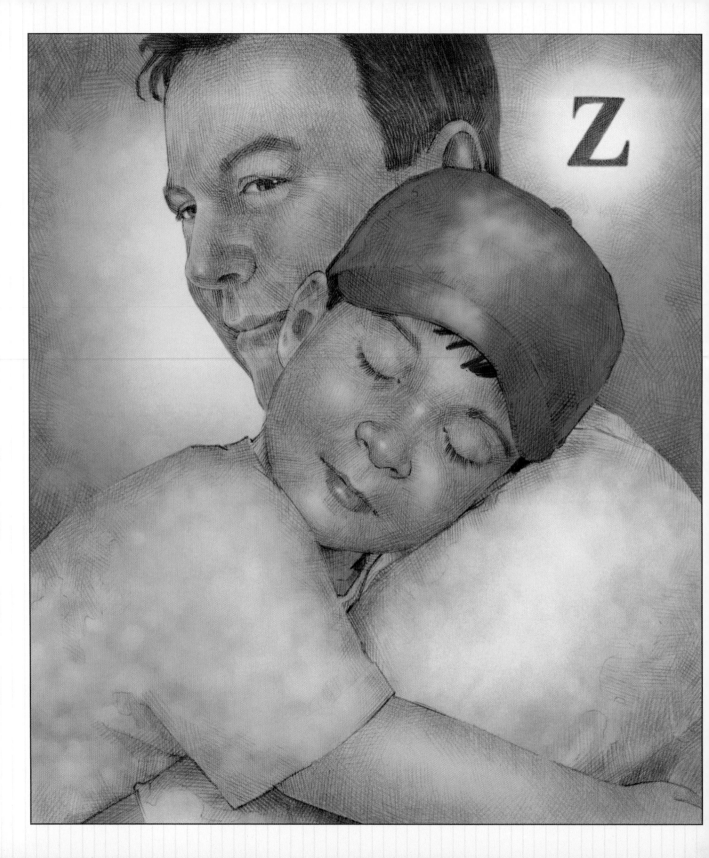

FUN FACTS

The statistics in this book are valid through the 2010 baseball season.

The Baseball

- About 70 balls are readied for play before each major league game.
- Approximately 600,000 baseballs are used by major league teams combined during the course of a season.
- One funny baseball rule is that before every game, umpires must rub mud and dirt on about six dozen balls to get rid of the shine on the new balls.

Pitch Grips

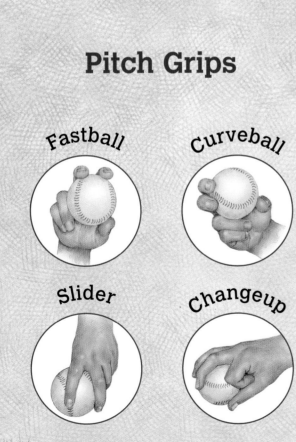

Fastball   Curveball

Slider   Changeup

Baseball Bats

- When baseball started, players brought their own bats to the game. They were all different sizes and shapes—there was even a flat bat used for bunting. But a seventeen-year-old boy has been credited with making the first bat that closely resembles today's. He worked in his father's woodshop in Louisville, Kentucky, and he made a bat for his favorite player, Pete Browning, when he broke his during a game.
- That bat was the first Louisville Slugger. The company continued to make bats for the likes of Babe Ruth and Ty Cobb, and today most Major Leaguers use Louisville Slugger bats.
- Bats can't be greater than 2½ inches in diameter, nor longer than 42 inches. Some players like heavier bats, believing that can propel the ball farther and other players like lighter bats, believing they can be quicker through the strike zone.

Sport

- Baseball cards appeared in 1868. Modern-day cards, with photos on the front and stats on the back, were introduced in 1953. Player photos are taken in the spring, with and without team caps, in case the player is traded to another team.
- The largest collection of baseball cards—200,000—is in the Metropolitan Museum of Art.
- The most valuable baseball card is of Honus Wagner of the 1909 Pittsburgh Pirates, who is widely considered to be one of the best players of all time. This rare card has been sold to collectors for more than a million dollars.
- The longest game in innings took place on May 1, 1920. It was 26 innings, but ended in a tie.
- Uniforms were first worn in baseball in 1849 by a team called the Knickerbockers.
- The National Baseball Hall of Fame in Cooperstown, New York, was created in 1935, the 100th anniversary of the game.
- Baseball stars from the National League

and the American League played the first All-Star Game in 1933. The American League won four to two. The National League has won 40 games, and the American League 38. There were also two ties, one in 1961 due to rain and one in 2002 due to lack of pitchers.

- The baseball tradition of spring training came about because in 1885 the Chicago White Stockings went to Hot Springs in Arkansas to prepare for the new season.
- The first World Series was played between Boston and Pittsburgh in 1903. Boston won five games to three in a best of nine.

Teams

- The Yankees have won more games than any other pro team in any sport. They have won the most league pennants and the most World Series.
- The Chicago Cubs have been dubbed Lovable Losers. They have not won a World Series since 1945. In the 1945 World Series against the Detroit Tigers, Billy Goat Tavern owner Billy Sianis brought his pet goat to the game and was asked to leave the ballpark because his goat was stinky. He left while saying "Them Cubs, they aren't gonna win no more." This is known to Cubs fans as the curse of the Billy Goat.
- The Boston Red Sox broke their own curse, the curse of the Bambino (which lasted 86 years) when they beat the Yankees in the 2004 ALCS four games to three. After losing the first three games, the Red Sox won the next four, winning the series. They went on to sweep the St. Louis Cardinals four games to none in the World Series. This feat had not been accomplished before.
- In 1935 the Cincinnati Reds beat the Philadelphia Phillies in the first major league night game under lights.
- The oldest Major League Baseball stadium still in use is Fenway Park, home of the Boston Red Sox.
- The Mets uniform pays homage to all teams that once played in New York (Giants, Dodgers, and Yankees).

Players

- In 1960 Mickey Mantle hit the longest home run ever recorded—643 feet.
- Lou Gehrig hit the most grand slam home runs, 23.
- In July 1934, Babe Ruth paid a fan $20 for the baseball he hit for his 700th career home run.
- Mickey Mantle of the New York Yankees holds the record for the most home runs hit during the World Series with 18.
- Pitcher Nolan Ryan holds the record for the longest career in baseball from 1966 to 1993.
- Mariano Rivera is the only active player wearing number 42. He was grandfathered in. Number 42 is a retired number in all of baseball in honor of Jackie Robinson.
- Baltimore Orioles shortstop Cal Ripken, Jr., didn't miss a game in sixteen years. He played in 2,632 consecutive games from May 30, 1982, to September 19, 1998.
- In 1941 Joe DiMaggio got a base hit in 56 consecutive games; this hit streak is the longest and has not been broken.

The Best of the Best

Pete Rose has the most career hits
4,256

Ed Walsh has the best lifetime ERA
1.816

Ricky Henderson has stolen
the most bases
1,406

Nolan Ryan has struck out
the most batters
5,714

Ty Cobb has the best
career batting average
.367

Barry Bonds has hit the most
home runs all time
762

Barry Bonds has also hit the most
home runs in a single season
73 in 2001

Baseball's Awards

Cy Young Award

The Cy Young Award is an honor given annually in baseball to the best pitchers in Major League Baseball, one each for the American League and National League. The award was first introduced in 1956 by Baseball Commissioner Ford Frick in honor of Hall of Fame pitcher Cy Young, who died in 1955. The award was originally given to the single best pitcher in the major leagues, but in 1967, after the retirement of Frick, the award was given to one pitcher in each league.

MVP Award

The Major League Baseball Most Valuable Player Award (MVP) is an annual Major League Baseball award given to one outstanding player in the American and National Leagues. Since 1931, it has been awarded by the Baseball Writers Association of America (BBWAA).

Silver Slugger Award

The Silver Slugger Award is awarded annually to the best offensive player at each position in both the American League and the National League, as determined by the coaches and managers of Major League Baseball. These voters consider several offensive categories in selecting the winners, including batting average, slugging percentage, and on-base percentage, in addition to "coaches' and managers' general impressions of a player's overall offensive value."

Gold Glove

The Rawlings Gold Glove Award, usually referred to as the Gold Glove, is the award given annually to the Major League Baseball players judged to have exhibited superior individual fielding performances at each fielding position in both the National League and the American League, as voted by the managers and coaches in each league.

AMERICAN LEAGUE

East

Baltimore Orioles
Oriole Park
at Camden Yards

Boston Red Sox
Fenway Park

New York Yankees
Yankee Stadium

Tampa Bay Rays
Tropicana Field

Toronto Blue Jays
Rogers Centre

Central

Chicago White Sox
U.S. Cellular Field

Cleveland Indians
Progressive Field

Detroit Tigers
Comerica Park

Kansas City Royals
Kauffman Stadium

Minnesota Twins
Target Field

West

**Los Angeles Angels
of Anaheim**
Angel Stadium of Anaheim

Oakland Athletics
Oakland-Alameda
County Coliseum

Seattle Mariners
Safeco Field

Texas Rangers
Rangers Ballpark
in Arlington

NATIONAL LEAGUE

East

Atlanta Braves
Turner Field

Florida Marlins
Sun Life Stadium

New York Mets
Citi Field

Philadelphia Phillies
Citizens Bank Park

Washington Nationals
National Park

Central

Chicago Cubs
Wrigley Field

Cincinnati Reds
Great American Ball Park

Houston Astros
Minute Maid Park

Milwaukee Brewers
Miller Park

Pittsburgh Pirates
PNC Park

St. Louis Cardinals
Busch Stadium

West

Arizona Diamondbacks
Chase Field

Colorado Rockies
Coors Field

Los Angeles Dodgers
Dodger Stadium

San Diego Padres
Petco Park

San Francisco Giants
AT&T Park

THE BASEBALL DIAMOND

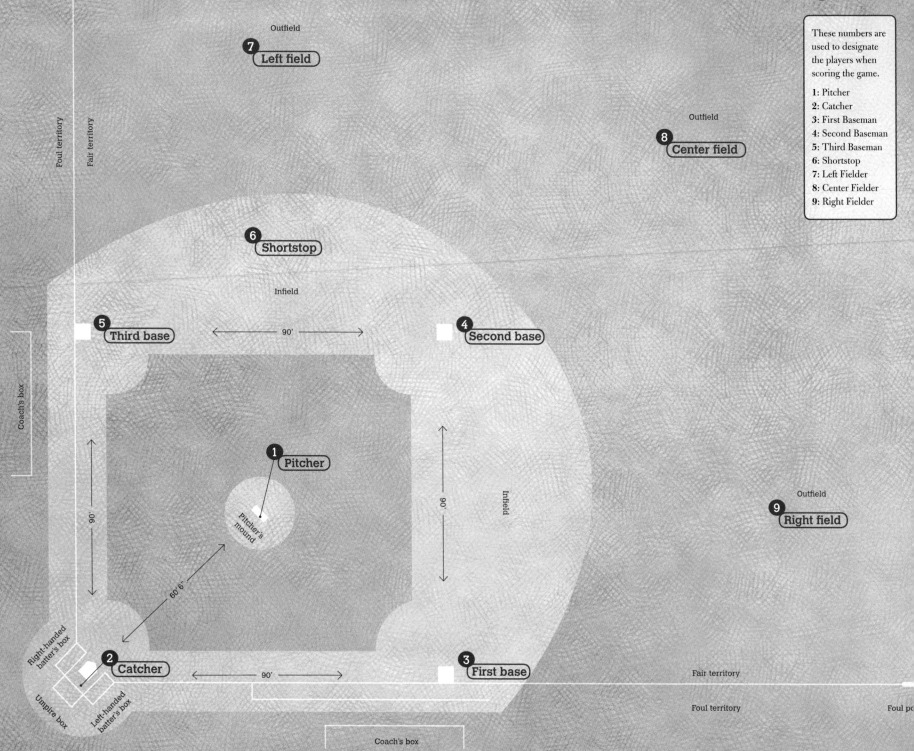

These numbers are used to designate the players when scoring the game.

1: Pitcher
2: Catcher
3: First Baseman
4: Second Baseman
5: Third Baseman
6: Shortstop
7: Left Fielder
8: Center Fielder
9: Right Fielder

Foul pole

Outfield

Foul territory

Fair territory

7 Left field

Outfield

8 Center field

6 Shortstop

Infield

5 Third base

90'

4 Second base

90'

Coach's box

Infield

9 Right field

Outfield

1 Pitcher

Pitcher's mound

90'

60' 6"

Right handed batter's box

2 Catcher

Umpire box

Left-handed batter's box

3 First base

90'

Fair territory

Foul territory

Foul po

Coach's box